THE NAMING OF CLOUDS

By the same author:

Poetry

G & S (with Tric O'Heare)
For the Record
The Bread Horse
Lucidity
Sjøvegen (The Sea Road (50 tanka for Ålvik)) English & Norwegian
The Blue Dressing Gown

Chapbooks

Light Travelling
Awakening—poems from the collection of the Castlemaine Art Gallery for the centenary
My Ship
Shh and other love poems
Tightrope Horizon

Educational

Kickstarting Poetry 1&2 (with Tric O'Heare)

THE NAMING OF CLOUDS

50 ghazals

ROSS DONLON

RECENT
WORK
PRESS
2015-2025
10 YEARS OF POETRY

The Naming of Clouds: 50 ghazals
Recent Work Press
Canberra, Australia

Copyright © Ross Donlon, 2025

ISBN: 9781763670129 (paperback)

A catalogue record for this book is available from the National Library of Australia

All rights reserved. This book is copyright. Except for private study, research, criticism or reviews as permitted under the Copyright Act, no part of this book may be reproduced, stored in a retrieval system, or transmitted in any form by any means without prior written permission. Enquiries should be addressed to the publisher.

Cover photograph and internal images: © Ross Donlon, 2025
Cover design: Recent Work Press
Set by Recent Work Press

recentworkpress.com
10 YEARS OF POETRY

For Tric O'Heare

Contents

Welcome to *The Naming of the Clouds*: A Foreword	1
Caravan	3
Dandelion	5
Racing	6
Acorn	7
The Trains	8
Children of War	9
The Days of Horses	11
The Quiet American	13
The Naming of Clouds	14
The Man with a Bucket	16
Child in a New Forest	17
Madonna	18
Apron	21
'We have heard the chimes at midnight'	23
The Flat in 1950	24
Bread	26
Butter	27
Knife	28
The Dance	29
We Ran Flying	30
Better than Anything	31
Pid	32
Self Portrait at Sixteen with Jack Kerouac	35
Scenes of Sydney	37
Vertigo	*38*
Afoot and light-hearted, I take to the open road	39
Swallows	41
The Horse	42
The Horses	44
Breath	45
Bringing Her Home	46
Growing Up With Donald Duck	47
White Cockatoos	49
Portal	50
The Sky Inside	51
In Radda	52
Ms Death	54
Echoes of Katoomba	55
paper remembers	56

The Being Here	57
Twilight	58
Reflection in London	61
Beach	62
Continental Drift	64
Water	65
Skin	66
Shirt Logic	67
Dreaming Awake	68
The Seas	69
My Ship	70

Welcome to *The Naming of the Clouds*: A Foreword

The Naming of Clouds, in its unique combination of aspects, very quietly subverts expectations. A book of memory, it forms itself through a combination of the ghazal poetic form with personal photographs and visual images. Line by line, image by image, the whole comes together revealing an examination of a long and thoughtful life. In this way, Donlon builds various worlds one poem at a time, inviting readers in to survey its unique landscape. The long line of the ghazal becomes the foundation on which these poems are formed—whole and apparent but also as ephemeral as clouds that might be named, with the power to catch the reader in a sudden storm of memories and corresponding emotions.

The ghazal's form inherently requires long lines and repetition which is apt for a work that represents a person's lifetime. These poems cover all matter of growing up in Australia—from poems about Donlon's childhood flat, to life with Donald Duck, to poems about boyhood holidays and a notable tree in a neighbour's backyard. It is through these deliberate detailed choices that Donlon fashions his worlds.

As the book builds its worlds, it also examines the tools that it uses to do so: words. Some poems, like "Bread," use the ghazal to contemplate words and their influence on our world. And the ghazal in its repetition at the end of the lines becomes the perfect conveyance for this type of contemplation.

The photos add shadowy images even as they illustrate and cast some light onto the words, and, at times, the images create juxtaposition. For example, the humorous poem about Pid. Alongside the poem, *The Poet's Pen* title page with A.K. Thomson's and Judith Wright's names and, drawn in, a peeking Pid, adds layers of perspective and delight.

Between the visual images and the poetic ones, in *The Naming of the Clouds* readers are invited into a place that is both distinctive and familiar, and that is part of this book's charm, where one thing is evident: the reader is wholly welcome to wander the long lines, savour the language, and have a good look around.

Kimberly K. Williams
Gladstone, Queensland

Caravan

From the Persian, karwan, 'a group of desert travellers'.

We trail from the rented holiday house, a linked caravan
of past & present, desert travellers in a tinkling caravan.

Pop leads in shorts, Messiah in Persil-white singlet & skin
weathered as leather. His boots make prints for our caravan.

It's a trek for all ages. Hills climb past grey, fibro cottages
set in sand & heat. Sleepy snakes watch a clinking caravan.

My widowed mother carries her book & a gay beach umbrella.
Nan follows later with lunch, her sandwiches & drinks caravan.

Cousin Jane & I tote buckets, spades, goggles & towels.
The sun floats egg-white, mirage of a flickering caravan.

After forever, sand dunes of a beach appear like the Sahara.
Tussocks shrink as time disappears from our shifting caravan.

Somewhere in and out of line, ghosts tramp weary headed,
merge then retire again to memory from a shrinking caravan.

The ocean appears, a sunken oasis. We slide down hills, thirsty
for its salty embrace. Waves roll chains of a shimmering **caravan (n):**

*originally from North Africa, Persia, Arabia, Crusaders' Old French
& Latin: 'Company of travellers going together for security*. Our caravan.

Here we are at lunch inside the paraphernalia of a typical post-war
holiday: Nan, Pop, Mum, my cousin & me, a time-blinkered caravan.

Walking back, the long day exhausted, my grandfather's heart pauses
to rest half way, Margin's Orange Ice Cream, his treat for the caravan.

The trail disappears like Arabian Nights with refuge in the rented house,
but the spell of family gathering is broken by loss and a missing caravan.

Dandelion

A widely distributed weed of the daisy family, with a rosette of leaves and large bright yellow flowers followed by globular heads of seeds with downy tuft. Late Middle English from French dent-de-lion *(because of the jagged shape of the leaves). A revered plant to the Ancient Greeks and Ancient Celts, sacred to Hecate and Brigid, the goddesses of homes, families and prosperity. Full bloomed dandelions were carried along with other bridal flowers to ensure happy marriages and big families. If you can blow all the seeds off a dandelion with a single breath, then the person you love will love you back.*

A small child knows none of these things. In the first garden the child sees dandelion seeds disappear before a breath. No words of love for the short life of the dandelion.

Beautiful, mysterious, ephemeral. No wonder tales of myth, symbol & spirituality rise from prehistory to today. Magic wand or weed? Janus face of the dandelion.

Dandy Lion is not etymological. Yet that's an image that prances forth knowledge-free, innocent as the need to have sex by the road. You bad seed of the daisy! You dandelion!

Love doesn't enter into it, except by way of parallel. Desire entices as it goes, silk seeds stick unwanted onto hands & clothes. One breath is never enough to woo the dandelion.

They knew irony, the ancients, wryly imposing lions' teeth on cloudy tufts, fragile, faint as air. Included in wedding feasts & floral bouquets, were there smiles for the dandelion?

I remember the counting & laughing faces of those above looking down as I blew. But I already knew I was loved that morning when the world was safe as dandelions.

Racing

In the backyard of a flat a boy carves out a track for racing.
Small, coloured plastic cars are all he has to begin racing.

He pulls up cape weed, buffalo grass and dandelion stalks,
a circle of dirt beneath the clothesline for invisible racing.

Invisible to adults. Women walk to and fro from the laundry
inside the copper's steam, mind on washing, blind to racing.

At ground level squinting, pebbles become boulders, sticks
become trees. He hand-rakes the track each time for racing.

The cars are plastic, finger-long, moulded with no wheels
in primary colours, pushed prodded and flicked to start racing.

One push-flick can never be just the same as another. Some
slew, others skim or slow down to avoid crashing while racing.

Winning is important for the blue and green, his favourite cars,
(so they do) but it's the pattern he looks to most while racing.

Camera eyes record above, below and alongside track views.
Touch adjusts aesthetic of race, shape and order of racing.

Solitary but mind-accompanied, a creative imagination grows
from car-play to word-touch to poems, my child's mind racing.

Acorn

The backyard was littered with bullet snubs of acorns
fired by an upstairs parent, the tree we called an 'acorn'.

Innocent inner city flat dwellers, no biology know-how
unpacked the mystery of the neighbour's exotic acorn.

And it was young then, slouched against the fence,
an adolescent clicking for attention. Lookit me. A.Corn.

But softer, its cup shaped cupule of indurated bracts
could be sweet gumnut babies in a nursery acorn.

Wars still thrived in the backyard since war fared
everywhere. *Ammo* was a cache of stockpiled acorn.

In time, of course, it became a sailing ship, just once
a mountain, prone to avalanche with falling acorns.

But as a ship full sail, breasting gusts of a Southerly Buster,
it's best remembered, cockpit sheering clouds of acorns.

Branches bent to the wind, veering over the neighbour's
into Eternity, I hung on howling in the thrash of acorns.

The oak it was eventually, never stayed true to memory.
Oaks are another story. In Sherwood. Ours was an Acorn.

The Trains

They wake your childhood then run away. Trains
make first moving pictures; the windows of trains.

On Sunday morning bed stories, Pop was fireman-
driver-hero hooting from a tunnel of rumbling trains.

Names galloped like stock from his country towns:
Wait-a-while. Junee. Harden-Murrumburra. Word trains.

On early excursions, subways echo something roaring
like thunder alive. Rumble of ghost trains.

Lodged at a window nose to glass, a child sees time
pierced by shining lines erased by tunnelling trains.

At the station, stairs climb skywards to platform cities.
Whistles shove crowds to the lottery of waiting trains.

Rattlers connect with chains like family. Carriages chat
and grumble into the city, race and jostle other trains.

Long trips make storybooks. A window pane is a page,
stations comics with cartoon characters. Tellers are trains.

I once rode from Canton to Helsinki hard-class sleeper,
washing in a bucket. Then a continent arrived by train.

Children of War

Bless all children at the moment of birth, but the child of war
bless more. Think to be born in trauma. Mourn a child of war.

Imagine a sky laced with fire, earth itself shaken to its core,
new mother crying with fearful joy, her infant defiled by war.

See (but you can't) the father's mind pierced with bullets,
shells yet to hit, longing and love denied, need stifled by war.

Friends and family who other times would gather close as a host
now scatter like rubble or hide inside it, their love sent wild by war.

My family survived but didn't. A ship took my father an ocean from us
broken. Bless all war children and children of those who die in war.

The Days of Horses

Grandfather lived his week for the days of horses.
I cut them from paper on a floor of torn horses.

He'd be propped up in bed, Old Man Mountain God
crumpled as form guides and sports pages of horses.

Linoleum stretched a green course around the room.
A mirror reflected the game of looking glass horses.

The radio sang its minaret song all Saturday long.
Race callers called ghost names of invisible horses.

A door suddenly opened could blow the field like fate,
skew the race. Paper shadows forgot they were horses.

God-in-bed rocked the springs. *Six to Four th' Field!
Two to One Bar One!* Bookies cheered for his lost horses.

The callers' word play made state of races a mystery.
Their chanting drummed the coming of racing horses:

*Rising Fast Tim Whiffler The Grafter White Nose Carbine
Comic Court Peter Pan Spearfelt;* the wordspell of horses.

Around and around they swept through my childhood,
first spoken word poems heard in the naming of horses.

The Quiet American

For my mother & father

He came to her from far away, from across the Pacific, the quiet American.
From jazz, comics, radio, romantic movies and pop culture, a polite American.

Even in uniform, private-corporal, corporal-private, his creams casual, elegant
as a Broadway star, tap dancing across the war to Australia, the right American.

And kind, she could tell, or convinced herself, and he was soft spoken, so unlike
her family's men, who could rip to anger quick as look, but this nice American.

It was passionate, she related, much later. Hard to imagine them in a clinch outside
her sister's home. Cue *Strings. Moonglow. Closeup.* Cut to a star-bright American.

Part of war in the Pacific, there's a wedding in St Vincent's. She's in her sister's gown,
He's disguised as a soldier. Soon a child makes its way to life, delight for an American.

War moves its pieces across the map of Papua, his snaps not much bigger than stamps.
Goofing with mates as she knits and waits. Japan dissolves in a bright light. Americans.

Every story has a beginning, middle and thread-tying end. The denouement in this case
is protracted. V for someone's victory. Love promises to return. The flight of the American.

The river is wide, says the popular song, *and I cannot cross o'er.* But an ocean is wider.
Like puppets they pull their strings, but snap. She dangles. He falls, a slight American.

Dying herself, my mother, seventy years later, I ask of him again. She still sees Bill,
she says, in dreams. They're both at a dance, but apart. In the twilight, an American.

The Naming of Clouds

For my mother

She remembered first day of school was *The Naming of Clouds*,
a moment still glimpsed like a sunbeam that came with the clouds.

Later that day there was maypole dancing, sewing & making a dress
she never wore. But her young mind had grown, retaining the clouds.

Other words came from outside school: spec fruit, broken biscuits, bread
& dripping, moonlight flits, the flight after dark through a game of clouds.

*We moved so many times. Between North Belmore & Belmore, Catholic
& public.* No money for Sport? Off to the Infants, shamed under a cloud.

Depression treats: a frozen orange thrown at a wall becomes an ice block,
meat pies peeled layer by exquiste layer, a contentment framed by clouds.

Dux of her class! A troop of nuns head down to the flat with magpie intent.
But fourteen means factories for working girls, the sameness of clouds.

Life creates our lexicons. Hers include: *war, soldiers, American, marriage,
son, widowhood, shop, office.* Yet beams of sun pierced rain filled clouds.

For there was dancing at *The Troc*, jiving with friends in dresses patterned
from *Butterick & Vogue*. A girl still turns before her mirror in a fantasy cloud.

Her decades deal good hands & bad, played with grace and hope. Cards
from friends and family arrive, one always missing, his remains under clouds.

I am heir to her life, the succour she found in family, music, books & film.
Words gleaned by her resilience made this poem from the naming of clouds.

The Man with a Bucket

Killcare, N.S.W. 1944

She tells the story of when he went shopping with a bucket,
strolling from their honeymoon beach armed with a bucket.

She's cut the legs of his army fatigues to make swim shorts,
so he paddles in surf, list in a pocket snug next to the bucket.

Their honeymoon home is a fibro shack hidden in sand hills,
but at night the moon shines back brimful in a silver bucket.

The beach near Sydney is called *Killcare* but they are care-less
then, as she sends him away splash-happy to shop with a bucket.

It's true, he sometimes becomes a mirage in the heat waving back,
or quite disappears in surf haze, almost a ghost clutching a bucket.

But after five days' leave the world reappeared. Back in its uniform
he marched to the dock and left, carrying kit instead of a bucket.

Like the first couple in Eden, my parents, in their Hollywood idyll,
in love on a beach with a wartime script, Bill acting a fool with a bucket.

Child in a New Forest

For my father

Once upon a time, a boy was lost in a dark forest,
where trees strode like giants, stark in the forest.

He became mist, dissolving into shadows and corners
searching for light and rescue, some spark the forest.

Wind startled leaves. Stars heaved, scrawling branches.
Birds soared from shadows, sudden marks in the forest.

Then he found treasure, the lost parts of a haunted soul
whose embers gleamed with hope, a shaft in the forest.

Beneath a crown, scepter and ring, a cloth covered book,
embossed gold on scarlet: *Children of the New Forest.*

Some pages were lichen yellow, some were uncut secrets,
a book buried when the coming of war startled the forest.

Like ghosts, letters hovered in words, each sentence a maze.
He touched images; golden children who larked in a forest.

Years passed. Sentences rose, crumbling time as he read.
A king's death. His specural shroud still dimmed a vast forest.

At last, through lines of sky, I saw a path made by words.
So I left my father and a park appeared that had been forest.

Madonna

Enter the boys-own not-centre page black and white photographs of Madonna, young naked porn limbs half open to the passive camera; playgirl Madonna.

First reference in *Firefox*, Google how you will. Start up your search engines you'll only find *Madge*. Madonna Louise Ciciccone, *Queen of Pop* Madonna.

In the Beginning, the word rocks out of the Beatles': *Baby at your breast, wonders how you manage to feed the rest?* But wasn't she someone's one-time lady, Madonna?

In a sepulchre shop window lines of plastic statues trademark downcast eyes, outstretched hands, piteous acceptance. Stereotypical import. China Madonna.

Somewhere in history she was fourteen, Joe her builder boy maybe rather older. Theologians and historians spin wheels of self-interest but what's lost is Madonna.

Poor wee girl, swallowed by a god. Or gods. Transformed by blind fate and faith into circus icon, Christmas card, Morning Star. But what about Mary, Madonna?

Next-to-central-figure in every nativity scene, each barn animal iconic, virgin womb borrowed for immaculate conception and Christmas delivery. A Blue Madonna.

Queen of Heaven with no King. *Mathew 1:19 Joseph, being a just man and not willing to make her a public example, was minded to put her away privately,* His ex. Madonna.

Spread below the cross like a blanket, the eyes uplift, asking? But no answer there from the gathering of grey clouds streaked with someone's heaven. *Pieta Madonna.*

Blue-cream plaster sorrowful statue in St Everywhere welcomes poor and penitent, *Our Lady* more working class sufferer than someone's martyr, a People's Madonna.

My mother's Go-To. Another woman who found trouble in war with men. Familiar face from childhood looking back sad, suffering and kind. My Madonna.

Apron

My grandmother stands at the kitchen sink of our small flat wearing her favourite apron.
Tied at the back, the loops too hard for a small boy to ignore. Granny knot of her apron.

Not bought but made. The singer pedal sewing machine rattles across cheap cotton cloth,
edges hemmed with a vibrant match. Red rick rack braid trims her black and white apron.

Solitary at the sink, small statue in after-hours of washing, peeling, cooking, wiping and putting
away. The long, grey, work skirt sways steps of a kitchen ritual. Solitary dance in a new apron.

Summer sunlight angles into the narrow window of the flat, turns sink suds into snowflakes.
But heat beats the kitchen like a gong. Baking his baked dinner, grease stains on her apron.

Fireside, winter's kerosene heater, cosy name with different connotations in small flat life.
Tripping not allowed for fear of Dante's *Inferno*. Stable for a clothes horse drying her apron.

Family departed. Alone at last but bereft, that family paradox. Children gone but left with his ghost.
Daily teacup and saucer, best too fine for breaking. Breaking nonetheless, falling from her apron.

A kind of hopscotch on the kitchen linoleum. Parkinson calls with respect. Short jumps into Hospital.

Hospital. Hospital. Nursing Home. *Bed-ridden*, that odd phrase. Independence gone with her apron:

A protective garment worn over the front of one's clothes, tied at the back. (We all need protection).
From Old French, 'naperon'. The 'n' in 'naperon' lost by wrong division. (Time will do that). Our apron.

Child point of view of an adult growing older. Nan's shanks narrow into worn slippers, varicose veins
bulge from a lifetime standing. I reach and undo the strings. Again, not looking up, she re-ties her apron.

'We have heard the chimes at midnight'

Falstaff, from Henry IV

The hardest chimes to hear are those which strike at midnight,
a sound when time ends time. Bells toll the death of midnight.

The heart rides each echo in the long, echoing cry of farewell.
Fear grows in every cell. Prayers try to stay alive at midnight.

Doomed ones know how precious time is between each chime.
The longest day ends at twelve. The sky opens wide at midnight.

Wolf hour. Witching hour. Brightest stars are light years away.
Moonlight ebbs with the tide. Life blooms and dies at midnight.

Race the dawn! How much can a day hold? Dreams are nightmare.
Past is present. Shutting in, dark draws down the mind at midnight.

As an invisible procession passed, Antony knew his time had come.
Alexandria! Unearthly music as the gods abandoned him at midnight.

Whatever minute our hearts break, convention allows a full day.
Penned, scratched or chiselled, time of death is always midnight.

Time watched as a young Queen knelt, fumbling for her blindfold.
Her women wept as History looked on, ready to strike at midnight.

The Flat in 1950

The newspaper feature said people who lived in flats
were 'losers'. We rented all our lives from rented flats.

So far as we could otherwise see were seas of houses,
terracotta-topped, chimney potted, blotting out our flat.

Those chubby houses claimed prime plots and squatted.
Edwardian snouts looked down and out at modest flats.

Houses shrub each other, cosily motor-mowing, trimming
a shared horizon, comfortably apart from a stray cat flat.

Language is cruel. *House* is a pleasant, soft-sounding word,
like *tousled mouse.* Flat sounds like itself. All rhymes lead to flat.

We strolled from our doors, relaxed as penguins on a tightrope.
Up and down we walked to train or bus. Cars rained on our flat.

Being actors, we acted normal. The snap, crackle and pop of life
entered without visas. Neighbours' yards are television from flats.

Good people, we strived to absorb their great depressions and world
wars. Our lives came and went easily as leases expiring in a flat.

At some point in the lexicon *unit* then *apartment* came without knocking.
One never charmed, the latter felt wealthy. Proud, we stayed in our flat.

Bread

Bread is the best word in English when you want bread.
One noble syllable, tasty in the mouth, serves for bread.

Reversing letters begin and end with a consonant crust.
Two round vowels hold the heart of hearth-made bread.

Flat as desert, moulded like hills or rucked like mountains,
geography and culture make exotic ingredients for bread.

Rhyming with primals like *head, bed, wed, fed and dead,*
no tricks and twists perplex the ear when you hear *bread.*

My bread rises with the sun. Like me, it's uneven and thick,
but tastes good loved up with a cuppa. I write honest bread.

Butter

Greek boutron joins *bous* (cow, ox) and *tyros* (cheese) to make our word for butter.
Cow's cheese might sound odd on the tongue, but that's the etymology of butter.

What do you think of when you think of butter? I think of Nan and a 'stick' *of Norco,*
something almost alive in the ice box, like a delicious piece of sun, or sin. Ah butter.

'50s memories. No butter bloke but there was the 'bread man'. Horse and cart parked,
he ran to the bread box where we waited like brigands, ready to mug hot bread with butter.

There we eschewed crust (later used to make snails) and dived into a wheat warm womb
slathered gold. With vegemite, honey or red jam, we added bliss to the blessing of butter.

The yellow block glowed in the ice box, an idol in a tabernacle, ready to add miracles
to Nan's cakes and scones, whatever the *Common Sense Cook Book* said for butter.

In other days, bread was graced with dripping, salt and pepper fresh from chops,
or after lamb had faced the griller, workers' treat in hard times older than butter.

Other employment comes shyly to mind. My friend's was shaving cream on a lover's pelt.
I dreamed of curious couplings with *Norco,* but could never wait for the butter to melt.

Knife

A word of unknown origin.

And perhaps origin is uncertain because we've lived so long with Knife. How soon after our first crawl did flint, shell and need take us to Knife?

Oldest tool. Oldest weapon. Which came first? Helping and hurting, protector and death-dealer in peace and war, the old history of Knife.

Blade varies with purpose and time. Culture curves or straightens. Ornate or utilitarian, it wears the wearer, heralds the bearer. My knife.

A voice can be a knife. Sharp words maime minds and slash hearts, transform moments into an end of days, the lasting effect of a knife.

I retrieved one, rusting in the past. So many had died other deaths. I cleaned and forgave it. Now it serves me well as a kitchen knife.

The Dance

Of remedies of love she knew per chaunce
For she could of that art the olde daunce—
                    The Wife of Bath – Geoffrey Chaucer

She koude of that art the olde dance
Bravo wife, bold in the timeless dance.

Love and dance, metaphor enhanced
as a couple entwined combine in dance.

The young vow to stay in time forever,
the old seek time to love and dance.

Ten thousand years ago dancers carved
us on their walls, no change in our dance.

My drug of life, precious as food and oxygen
and will to go on, pilgrim in this primal dance.

We Ran Flying

It was a time when boys never knock but gather outside your flat, ready for flying.
Someone shouts to make you look and there wait Ric & Moose, revving for flying.

Dusk has begun. Night flows a draught over beds getting infants ready for sleep,
but adolescence flicks ignitions on the engines of us on an evening perfect for flying.

Footpaths become runways, street lights line a hilly tarmac as we ease into formation,
agree on a secret flight path across yesterday's suburb, starlit course cleared for flying.

Soaring into sky as sun sets, we rise higher as the glare of day fades into its hanger.
Night takes over, turning a training run for House Aths Carnival into a time for flying.

Sixteen. Old enough to be 'let out at night', the phrase reminiscent of something caged
released into air and we are, sandshoes become wings, aligned and primed for flying.

Above the disappearing streets and invisible roads we rise, sublime as gods on holiday.
Dusk becomes night, searchlights rove looking for boys/almost men/ still children/ flying.

Sixty years on in another flight through space, the sensation returns, a dream relived,
weightless thrill of youth one summer evening lifting us from the future, free and flying.

Better than Anything

After the jazz composition by Bryce Rhode

When you're young you have to emulate something, some style or persona better than you think you are; clothes, hair, mind, lens, anything to make you feel better.

At school forever by day, uniformed but tie loosened, blazer slung, your undone self is half out of class in the unconscious stream of the highway & you're better.

At night, city lights of shops, traffic & neon flash a Morse-like code to the young, duffle coats pegged to disguise shy youth beneath. The sun is gone for better.

Day feet in school leather now tread streets in suede desert boots / brothel creepers, yet we know nothing of deserts nor brothels, sloping along cool, dreaming of better.

Street life sings night. Life bursts living banks inside you. Each breath is a tenor sax solo. Inhalation converts experience into expression, outbreath a sense of better.

For a time my mind was light as neon. Music & poetry blew a gale of words spoken, typed or scribbled as Saturday night chapters built my own city, a palace better,
      or so it seemed, and still does, than anything.

Pid

He came from pages of schoolboy time in texts too decrepit for moths, Pid.
Latin primers taught more dead than alive by *Snake* were enlivened by Pid.

In a lame attempt at responsibility, a grid compelled boys to write *Name Year*
inside a cover (if there was one) useless as declining verbs by rote but for Pid.

His pudding nose looped over chapter headings into nothing, sausage fingers
hooked into chapters asking, *Why?* Eyes pinpricked. Question mark for hair, Pid!

The more you saw, the more you could see him. An adoptive parent reliable as
Pid Woz Here salved initiation into First Year, a cheeky spirit, friendly ghost, Pid.

Taken under his wing, safe inside the maelstrom of sometime sadistic masters
who threw chalk, twisted ears, *Donlon! Six of the Best!* we revenged, thanks to Pid.

Pid Woz Here struck back on toilet walls & locker doors smashed to practise karate.
Older brother, disgraced uncle, disowned cousin or mate, life had purpose with Pid.

No mystery to find his antecedent memes in other conflicts: *Foo* (Forward Observation
Officer) in **WW** I, *Kilroy & Chad* in II, *Smoe, Clem, Sapo, Flywheel* et al. But we had Pid.

Q. *What do they have in common?* A. *They are ahead of where anything should be*. Men
storming a beachhead were relieved to see *Kilroy was Here* already protecting, like Pid.

Only child & younger than others, the typhoon of uniforms, ties, prefects, fights & Houses
spawned by principal's names called on wit, rat cunning & a subversive following of Pid.

Where is he now? Long vanished into schoolboy dreams, he returns now. Magoo-like
he hangs over the back fence of my mortality, knowing eyes & nose waiting. Cheers Pid.

THE POET'S PEN

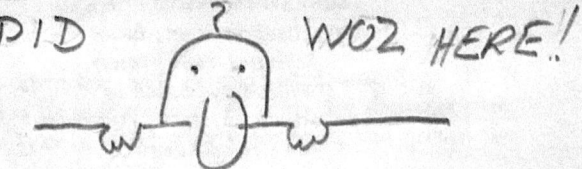

COMPILED BY

A. K. THOMSON

AND

JUDITH WRIGHT

THE JACARANDA PRESS

Self Portrait at Sixteen with Jack Kerouac

The night you leave your suburb behind you is like leaving fifteen for sixteen.
Stairs from subways rise to the tornado of Emerald City. Red sneakers at sixteen.

Friday night could be Christmas or New Year. Traffic lines jam intersections, head-
-lights roam the crowd of nightwalkers. Light and dark is about to start at sixteen.

Each pub is its own theatre, three act plays in every corner. Cracked cream-
-green tiles awash with beer stream teenage certainty, vomit and blood at sixteen.

Too young to drink legal, the illegal thrill rises like bubbles on heads of beer
and you. Light as a balloon inflated by being still half-boy, you fly high at sixteen.

Williams Street climbs to invade Kings Cross, its neon horizon of adulthood
collision of worlds. Calvary waits as you bear the rough cross of being sixteen.

Jack Kerouac trudges ahead in jeans and chequered shirt from *The Dharma Bums*.
Acolyte, you follow his trail of jazz and poems with the desolation of being sixteen.

The night ends with a week's pocket money gone in a taxi. You wake to a chorus
of lawnmowers. Yet how beatific to feel beat, just shy of being beautiful, at sixteen.

Scenes of Sydney

By night Sydney harbour is circled by a coronet of diamonds.
Wave crests fleck blue to white, slashed and star-cut by diamonds.

These might be ferries or other busy shipping, moored or moving.
High-rise towers of the rich shimmer reflections of glittering diamonds.

Sydney can be a hard town. Kings Cross lends its name to metaphor
easily. It's hard to turn right. In the gutter, chips of moonlit diamonds.

On endless nights old streets obey colonial mapmakers, curve above
indigenous streams and gullies to the Tank Stream's hidden diamonds.

Each day the traffic snakes in, shedding skin to the hammers of breakfast
jocks. Rail commuters wake to the roar of metal and sun-blazed diamonds.

Beyond Sydney, outer suburbs hedge their bets and look to the mountains.
Postcard swims are far away. In winter, rugby flags of bristling diamonds.

Explorers' trails from Parramatta River turned scrub into a suburb. Ashfield.
Arising from terra cotta, *Peek Frean's* biscuit factory, the scent of diamonds.

I spent my youth there, anxious to get to the harbour, where life real began
(I thought) anywhere there east of west, callow with my rough cut diamonds.

Vertigo

Condition in which a person has the sensation of movement or of surrounding objects moving when they are not.
Movie by directed Alfred Hitchcock with James Stewart & Kim Novak. Music by Bernard Herman.

Sometimes a word looks & sounds as dangerous as itself. The Capital V in Vertigo introduces the condition like a knife, leads its victim's fall to oblivion from Vertigo.

Surreal sensation of objects floating in a fantasy world disconcerting as Wonderland. Here, a chair not there anymore, a cup & saucer floats like a boat drowning in Vertigo.

Or is it like love? The lonely mind loses its horizon as gravity becomes vertical. Hearts heaving with a longing to be normal, revolve in dizzy orbit around Vertigo.

In the movie, caught-off-balance James Stewart slips as Kim Novak unhinges his mind, leading him to a past where both will die in the present from Vertigo.

Bernard Herman's score recalls Wagner. Think *Tristan & Isolde* for Jimmy & Kim, lovers marked by something worse than fate as their universe falls into Vertigo.

Too young, I watched a simple, earnest man keep falling & falling as love struck, once in sham and twice in reality to leave him broken, a lesson I forgot from *Vertigo*.

Afoot and light-hearted, I take to the open road

From Walt Whitman, Song of the Open Road

Afoot, my friend Dave and I tramp across rivers and Singapore bridges, hitching to
 far Penang.
We raise shy thumbs, happy to breathe pre Lee Kwan Yew sewerage on *The Road
 to Penang.*

Light-hearted? Yes, light as two twenty year old friends can be in early 1965.
 We've skipped war
in Vietnam under cover of being on-leave public servants to test our manhood
 hitching to Penang.

Across the causeway and strait into Malaysia we rucksack, quite careless of the
 traffic phalanx,
its early cacophony, thrilling to first time sights, sounds and smells, bound north
 for far Penang.

Somewhere on the nearby coast is Changi, a name clanging like prison bars from
 POW stories.
Stoic soldiers inform and strengthen our adventure as we risk rides merely to reach
 Penang.

There must have been lifts, for we are open-faced and innocent, green as a tropical
 summer.
Our years shine like fresh spray from a wave rolling the Pacific all the way north
 to far Penang.

The rides come, constant as curiosity. Our drug of preference is being alive,
 thrilling to the exotic.
Each temple, house, roadside stall or gathering is cornucopia for senses striving to
 reach Penang.

Colour riots with the aroma of incense in Malacca. Pretty pink and white
 buildings from Portuguese

in peaceful city squares. Powerful curries and gun shots at night produce excited
smiles. To Penang!

K.L. and the heat equatorial. We stand alert as statues in sunglasses, dripping sweat.
Rides rumble
into traffic past playing fields and mosques majestic. We rake into the city, a day's
hitch to Penang.

Arrival! But now my bosom companion Dave from Barrow and I will part. He
will hitch his way
unbroken across the half-world. My way to see other friends globe-dotted, leads
from Penang.

South, ever south, shining new seven league boots survive a solo road to
Singapore, then ship
for Hong Kong, hard class sleeper to Beijing, Ulan Bator, Moscow and Helsinki,
far from Penang.

Afoot, alone but hope-hearted, I hitch from Helsinki to Stockholm to Oslo. A
Sydney stripling
hails Vikings on Independence Day, 17th May. Cars hurry to host me a hostel far
from Penang!

A lifetime of travel trails into the ether of Eternity. Lucky to carry the confidence
trick of being
a boy, lucky to make man. Our risk in the sixties was death, worse, our sisters'
Road to Penang.

Swallows

For Sylvia Brogo

From the hollow of winter comes a flight of swallows,
a shape, opaque at first, that flows into swallows.

The valley is wide with olive groves and lines of vines,
leaves in motley but shadowed by crossing swallows.

Snow shimmers from the silhouette of distant mountains,
glitters on lines of vines and villas which house swallows.

It's a shard of time in a Tuscan landscape, the being here
simple and profound, as evening slows to a flight of swallows.

The flock begins as a wisp of smoke, then expands to lace
unraveling as they feed on invisibility, a host of swallows.

At last they cover the sky like a fable from childhood,
of a child lost, then found, by a flock of billowing swallows.

The Horse

When I read that the human population has reached 8 billion I think of the horses who led us from creation. Eohippus by a head. First past the post were horses.

Predators only to grass and low hanging leaves, their hunger is for speed & flight. Their strength is in endurance & being able to run like morning light, to be horses.

Then us. Our 'horse-drawn' era turned a creature into a machine, caught, broken, caged, harnessed, trained as a servant of war, farming & industry; 'working horses'.

Nineteenth century capital cities in old worlds and new rang to clatter, clang, cry, crack, steel-shod lightning & thunder crashed from carts & carriages pulled by horses.

Around this cruelty, coliseums of stables spiralled into the smoky sky. Babel Towers shouted in all languages & dialects surrounding slave cells of imprisoned horses.

Race & steeplechase dirt-sand-grass rail-curved tracks still urge small men's shining silk stretching colours along necks of whip & iron chastened horses.

Don't wonder why myths turned our lust & longing into centaurs & centaurides. Muscled torso, commanding gaze & arched back ripple our longing to be horses

How the history of humans on earth can be condemned by our relationship to this animal. I look in wonder at their pace, power & nature and wish our world were ruled by horses.

The Horses

For Kristin Holst

Three twelve-year old girls have turned into horses,
but hold onto reins, being riders as well as horses.

Cantering in circles through tall summer grass,
they wind the spell that turns girls into horses.

And now there is song, a climbing helix of notes
a phoenix might call to a troup of passing horses.

So primal, this need to feel freer than humans can be,
to run faster, fly higher, beyond the self – to be horses.

In the park there are ramps left by skateboarders
but the girls find jumps just made for three horses.

Two take turns to lie still as water and the third props
before she leaps into air – the kindness of horses.

Heads erect, their pony-tails catch the bobbing sun.
I watch from another time, as one should with horses.

Breath

For Gwyneth & Cosima

Nine months kept alive by blood from your mother's heart to a breath
of hospital air, the universe alters from inside to out, all in one breath.

Birth came with a tap, one of five senses first to react as they connect
to life outside the womb. Vital signs light up, flashing from one breath.

Your lungs, long dormant, wake pitch perfect, finely tuned as any voice
set for recital. First performance, first composition all sung in one breath.

Your costume is swaddling, ancient as birth itself. Did a wardrobe mistress
wait in the wings with props, alert for her cue, the first song of one breath?

I write from first photographs as your new grandfather, see my daughter's
soft smile of maternity as you inhale the same air, two breaths in one breath.

Bringing Her Home

For Gwyneth

She was so small that when she lost a dunny race with her twin sister at grandparents' home
she lost a baby tooth as well, falling or being shoved into the toilet bowl in the sprint for home.

Small enough to be in a nappy, snaggle tooth broken like a vampire's fang, the rest of her bright
as a pup, cute as a cufflink, curlytop hair the despair of a comb, the youngest child of our home.

It had to go, the stalactite sharp as a knife inside her mouth, odd-one-out in a line-up of tiny teeth,
so it was doc, hospital & op, then overnight the children's ward, her first time away from home.

We fretted, as though she'd taken both our hearts with her. Green gowned strangers took her away
& we slept awake while night seeped into morning & anaesthetic took her dreams to another home.

Anxiety raised visions of her frightened & calling out to us in an empty ward, nurses distracted,
flashing lights red ringing emergency & her marooned in an island cot far away from her home.

My car on silent siren took me in, convinced I'd find her crying but found her performing for nurses,
proud of the *prickle in her bum-bum*. So I gathered her up in the ship of myself & sailed her home.

Growing Up With Donald Duck

After years of self-analysis I still don't know why I lack a temper
but it might explain my attraction to Donald Duck and his holy temper

For he's most things I'm not: manic, vain, selfish, greedy, self-absorbed
(I did say *most*) but I love that bill-reverberating quack. What a temper!

Think of the pantheon of Walt Disney cartoons and comic strip characters,
imprinted like a negative on a child's vacant mind, just one with a temper.

Not Mickey Mr Squeaky-Voice-Fixit, all grin-and-button- Big-Ears, never fazed
by danger. Depression era hero, he wins by his smarts, never with temper.

But Oh, Donald Fauntleroy Duck. Near unintelligible in his pompous rave,
top half sailor suit, bow tie, rakish cap, cocky strut and nuclear temper.

And no pants. That white tuft of cheeky tail is a statement salute in itself.
He loves life with a grin, loses heart to begin, then fires up his temper

and wins! Bullies and Beagle Boys, the fickle, unforgiving Finger of Fate,
fall away before the tsunami torrent of dear Donald Duck's tsunami temper.

War hovered then, set for a choice between Mr Nice Guy and Mr Duck.
But I tell my kids, *Be silk and steel, velvet in the iron of your temper.*

White Cockatoos

Dotting morning trees like perky meringues, a mob of white cockatoos
wake workers with their shark's cry of *White Cockatoo! White Cockatoo!*

Wheeling through air from the wrong side of town, the bad boy & girl birds
bash trees, riding Sky Harleys under sulphur helmets badged: *White Cockatoo.*

Sleep is murdered & dreams are polka-dot nightmares of staccato calls
as they rattle clouds, use trees as trampolines & chant the *Rule of the White Cockatoo.*

Life is their orgy. Greedy claws & cheeky beaks snatch & grab from the orchard's
boring rows, every branch ruptured by Monsieur Connoisseur White Cockatoo.

Sheiks of summer, their robes unfurl with more abandon than Lawrence of Arabia
could ever twirl on a train (& with more insight) just happy to be a white cockatoo.

Heaven's big top, be it starched grey, circus stripes or panoramic blue, is the set
for its stars, The Lords of Misrule, skylarking for poor us - who are not white cockatoos.

Earth needs these outriders, scouts at the edge of the black-holed universe, warrior-clowns
who live long as humans (but upside-down) Dis-Orderers of Australia, The White Cockatoo!

Yet at rest on a waving branch after another day's drama, some inner self glows like crystal.
Sheathed like monks, they nod in contemplation, seeking the *Way of the White Cockatoo.*

I love them, my shadow self & totem & rejoice each day in their cartoon drama,
hoping to rise with their fire to an afterlife clowning with white cockatoos.

Portal

i.m.

He was *working on his soul,* he said, as he began to leave the portal
of life, fading from his hospital bed towards another, distant portal.

He was one of us, ones who see the world somewhat askance
through words, that fusion of thought and feeling, a poets' portal.

There, moons swing like coins on the sun's necklace, the spheres' music
calls to souls, meteorites shower a violet light, star path to the last portal.

Carpe diem. Yet how many days can a life hold before the hands atrophy?
The mind returns looking for clues, celestial detective casing a star's portal.

Even the word emerges like a ghostly shape trying to find itself: *gate,
passage, refuge, port,* a *place where ships may shelter from storms:* portal.

Each friend's death diminishes and enhances us. We grow with love,
join his ship sheltering in stars, before he sails alone to a waiting portal.

The Sky Inside

i.m.

The myth of Daphne is far removed from Joanna, of *The Sky Inside,*
her journal of work and love and way of looking at the sky, inside.

She was no dweller in Acadia by the river Ladon, no god pursued her
egged on by Cupid's curse, but her forever love lives in the sky inside.

Not the quick clutch of lust which masquerades as love, theirs ran river
and story book deep, years like a constant stream, like the sky inside.

He was maker, she dancer, in their world of timber, music and light, day
and night the only sense of time beneath the cosmos of their sky inside.

But cancer has no sense of time. It comes, arriving like a kind of fate,
unearned, undeserved. It grows plant-like but never like the sky inside.

In the aftermath, she continues, sustained by love, memory and grace.
The light of lost love grows within her now, nourished from the sky inside.

In Radda

for Silvia Brogo

For two hours the bus climbs in and over hills from Florence to Radda, hilltop town in Chianti. Postcard romance is charmed by reality in Radda.

Amphitheatre sky, tiny pepper-pot town sustained by hills, once war fodder between Florence and Sienna. Now statues and vines lead you to Radda.

In Tuscan summers wild boars snuffle, root in ruins and woods. Lined groves rollercoast hills. The past is close as an Etruscan shard waiting for you in Radda.

At night, wilderness barks back at hills. Animals retake the dark as the moon wakes villas, silvers pools. In a stone garden, an horizon of towers guard Radda.

The sun leaps from hills like a deer. Dawn surrounds with bird sound. Cockerels wake cars, then cafes. Dusk is slow to leave. Drinks touch on a terrace in Radda.

Hills approach and recede, a kind of time tide. Heat still rises from Roman stone. *Panna cotta* ends evening on a terrace. Tomorrow's plans are stardust in Radda.

Memory, my restless ancestor, merges with the landscape. Familiarity and friends beat the heart like a drum. Hills fit like a jigsaw, this unlikely piece home in Radda.

Ms Death

Summer in Rome. Crowd confetti with gelato, plazas packed to death.
Tourists transit from one world to another and slouched on a step, Death.

Heat hovers its mirage above the square. Crucifixes horizon the seven hills.
Tourists glisten with sweat, but one face is pallid with the afterglow of death.

Eternity in each eye, greased skull and cheeks, straight line lips painted black,
a hoodie hangs over skinny jeans and Doc Martens, a skeleton bored to death.

The scythe might be a broomstick from another time. Black plastic tape flutters
wryly from its blade, but something surreal suggests she's the real deal, Ms Death.

A cardboard coffin wobbles lightly on its stand above a white, polystyrene cup,
her ironic nod to life. Then she drains a last fag, more Death-warmed-up than Death.

Standing, she gazes lighthouse-like across the plaza, raking for likely souls, anyone
cruising on the edge of the cosmos feigning invisibility (or invincibility) from death.

No John Keats, but still a poet sick in Rome, teetering on the edge of breakdown
between Vatican and Colosseum, mind typing SOS, I blink and back winks Death.

It's a sudden sense of looking into life's last black hole, outer space becoming inner
without the star trek, then familiarity of going home at least to comfort and rest in death.

But I break my eyes, feel my life snap and rock as cortisone kicks. There are lucky
beads to buy, scenes to see of someone's idea of heaven, and a god nailed to death.

Echoes of Katoomba

Original indigenous name, Kedumba or Katta-toom-bah: shining water falling or water tumbling over hill

Tourists sprout selfie sticks and pose by panoramas, cliffs and falls. Katoomba snaps lookout heads. But the *Three Sisters* are still cloaked in stone in Katoomba.

A plethora of place names: *Shining Water Falling, Water Tumbling Over Hill, The Crushers, William's Chimney, Collett's Swamp*, but since 1877 all names drained to *Katoomba*.

The town's stats list vital vistas of excess. Out of sight numbers for cults, home-school, unemployed, mentally ill, homeless, held by the spell and spiel of Katoomba.

En route to haunted guest houses, suburbs run a sideshow to entertain the train. The living leave Central via backyard sociology en route to the show at Katoomba.

At Echo Point, watchers lean into an abyss waiting time to return a call if it chooses. Is the relayed voice younger, older or another self, locked in rocks beneath Katoomba?

Clouds, trees, shadows and sunlight make mountain reflections in blue water. Shape shifting drifts of misty air draw veils of mystery over ghosts of Katoomba.

From the Jamison Valley winds holler *Cooees* from lost or playful bushwalkers. An amphitheatre of silent sound mourns phantom tribes rising to Katoomba.

The town's streets cascade to tourist views, rollercoaster perfect postcards and memories, haunting us like *The Shining* - if we escape from Katoomba.

paper remembers

flocks of birds passed, a rustle of paper
birch trees fluttered gold leaves of paper

she said insects live in maps of bark
trees live eons on sheaves of paper

they read the sky each morning
lines of love fading on blue paper

their song heard again for the first time
her voice drew notes across the paper

a mind's imprint watermarked each day
held to the light a face rose from paper

some words echoed on cards letters
notes and books – then silence on paper

they entered, met, wrote on each other
left names on air and scraps of paper

The Being Here

Lying together as winter breathed, the being here seemed simple and profound, yet how strangers become lovers is always a mystery, both simple and profound.

The night began with hesitation and hope but ended in loss, since one stayed while one flew away. It's a common lovers' equation, both simple and profound.

Pages kept turning of course, but in the rush of days some remain blank, unsent, erased or forgotten. It's a paradox that love can (or can't) be simple and profound.

Songs eased pain on lonely nights but music is someone else's cry to the sky. When looking glass stars reflect separate lives it's a fact, simple yet profound.

Were there texts or Skype? Yes. But that contact is light as confetti compared to the spell of human touch. Distance + Time = Loss. It's simple and profound.

I remembered the couple in Larkin's poem, two effigies holding hands in stone, bodies in another dimension. Like us, it's a timeless separation. Simple. Profound.

Twilight

The dead are invisible, not absent.
—St. Augustine

It's twilight here but perhaps for you still night,
my love, writing your poem of grief each night.

Your bedroom will be dark, all windows locked,
curtains drawn to block out light, rescue night.

The house is wound around your heart in a maze.
Only you know where threads lie strewn at night.

Your nightgown, 'your gown of night', white lace
patterned in tiny stars, glows pale blue ghost at night.

Perhaps for now you live in reflection, day bright
with illusion, grieving in lieu of sleep each night.

Day revives memory, shock of the sudden loss.
I wait til sunlight dies, watch over you by night.

I remember pale shoulders turning from me
like the moon's last phase, the purity of night.

Even here, time passes. Sorrow, like moonight,
grows then fades, but love is constant as night.

Reflection in London

There are three photographs of him, images in a window in London,
roads wet in the square, passers-by somewhere anywhere in London.

He doesn't hide the camera phone, although it becomes quite invisible
in the flash of making an image of a man waving at nothing in London.

There must have been a gap or two between shots since the red van left
stage left and a new set of strangers bent against a sudden shower in London.

Everyone is purposeful, jackets and hair blown as they stride this morning
to work, an engagement or headed for home. He might be alone in London.

No one notices as he raises a phone before his face like a shield, or a pass
to enter something waiting to happen in another time and place in London.

Behind the man, but facing the window reflection, taxis and other traffic nudge
themselves. There's bunting across the street, sign of a mystery play in London.

Slim and athletic, sports top and vest projecting indifference to weather, expression
expressionless, he's focused on the task of a moment, to be moments ago in London.

In Stockholm, Oslo and once at a play in Melbourne, I took similar photographs, front
and centre of life as a landscape in time rushed by, a living statue there and in London.

Beach

Each night, leaving his settled family in camp, he makes his way to the beach,
the bush black & white with moonlight for his assignation on an empty beach.

Washing up done & put away, his wife & children sit by the campfire chatting.
Their circle glows with holiday happiness as he finds his way alone to the beach.

It can't be dangerous, but could be, this walk, the dark trees bright with sounds
& music he doesn't understand, distracted by time & a night walk to the beach.

Why is it that this track feels more like a wide river, stretched from home hearth
into space? Stars don't connect like they do in charts. All that waits is the beach.

Shadow shapes of trees flicker from a sea breeze. A lighthouse sweeps across
the phases of his life, a familiar phantom-proton joining plankton on the beach.

Somewhere behind is the spine of land, shape of a distant story that bulks large,
a monument to the day. How far does time stretch, from birth to night on a beach?

Beyond the breakers and waves weaving tapestry is the Pacific, endless as Eternity.
Naked, he is pale as moonlight entering the wash, then swims away from the beach.

Continental Drift

The children leave like continents
leaving Gondwana, the first continent.

The Old World splits like an atom,
becomes *Incognita*, an unknown continent.

Climate changes. Oceans rise,
drowning memories of a continent.

Evolution turns another way. Land
bridges dissolve, marooning a continent.

Where is landfall with so much land fallen?
Will an horizon ever return to this continent?

Where they were the coast is not clear.
I tell the history of an aging continent.

Water

A clear fluid, without colour of taste, that falls from the sky as rain and is necessary for animal and plant life
        From O.E. *wæter,* Latin *unda* (wave) and Greek *hudōr* (water)

And without it. Nothing. Falling from the sky, predicted or not, life giving water takes life away, blessing and curse older than naming, falling like rain to water.

The flood in the womb made of blood, new foetus floats nourished and embraced. Its tide rises from months of weather. Then the child makes berth in a body of water.

First maps make coast and river more important than roads. Arteries of the world's body pump life into death, surround land like a fickle lover. *The Sea Road* is water.

Migrations flood it. Refugees roll lives across it like dice. Smugglers and pirates use waves as camouflage. Submarines dive like whales - a pollution of water.

On some nights it's strange to think how maps contract both land and sea. *Space Ships* embark in vainglorious power, sailing across sky endless as water.

I swim each morning in a reservoir, *a place where something is kept in store.* That something being kept is its soul - and mine - in this meditation on water.

Skin

We want to make love to the water's skin
slip inside it, through the black & white skin
of night water, parting gold & sable petals tenderly as skin,
submerging ourselves in its midnight skin,
in a moment of pure, elemental love, someone's skin
being rainbows of dark champagne faintly bubbling over skin
& stars, which fall like rain from the blueness of space, that inner & outer skin.

How can we not swim in a gentle, turning, gyrating movement of stroking skins
in & out as we cross open water, changing position to accommodate each other's skin,
the passive, placid water winding around us, ruffling the fine hair on our skin,
& the moon billowing across the surface, so yes, let's romance it, the skin
of the moon, 'moonskin', as they say in the north, covering earth & sky in its pale skin
like armadas of galleons, heavy with hope, their wavelet & spinnaker skins
cutting the surface & journeying the thoughts of a man & woman, whose skins
spread two wakes which have led to a moment at midnight in each other's skin
& full moon-time is no time like any other time in the still water's centre, a skin
where lovers rest before kissing & breast-stroking, then dressing to go home & sleep, skin
to skin into skin.

Shirt Logic

They history your wardrobe, taut almanac of shirt
logic, draped like fashion skeletons in a row of shirts.

Daily existential dilemma of self. Who am I today?
Dress to impress or loose as a goose in a shirt?

The better halves live upstairs, backs iron-straight
swaying shyly at air of any interest in a shirt.

Moved in exasperation, someone shouts, *Pants!*
but you will never hear as an ejaculation, *Shirts!*

Like centaurs, they contain our chest, our heart.
We heave emotion through the armour of a shirt.

Cellar dweller slacks stay pressed and repressed,
fold in on themselves looking skywards to shirts.

Favourites, like all favourites, can wear themselves
out. The top button is always undone on my shirt.

Dreaming Awake

Before an open window and night's silhouette of trees, dreaming awake,
a cool touch arrives like a guest as if something else is near, dreaming awake.

So perhaps the old maps are right, and somewhere a face with streaming hair
has sent a breath in kinship, caressing the mind while we're dreaming awake.

Half inside time's looking glass, half beneath a Plimsoll line of consciousness,
the heart counts in a cave dark with hope, fear and longing, dreaming awake.

Five senses explore five ways of staying alive, while the sixth and coxswain,
directs a pulse each night of the year, rowing night into day, dreaming awake.

After eighty orbits through the firmament, patrolling dark and light,
these six pull me ashore each day and I rise. Until then, I'm dreaming awake.

The Seas

The view from a top floor flat is far from the coast, the sky its own sea,
rear bedroom window a lookout, mind free as night clouds on the sea.

Backyard roofs & fences are easily waves, street tree tops are flickering
white caps in the wind, crescent sails of a galleon, moon in an old sea.

Far beyond the fading blue horizon, Norfolk pines rattle creaking masts,
harbour moored in Ashfield Park. Ships rock, now safely home from sea.

Edges fade between sea & sky. Tides roll in, taking over. Mists dim the edge
of horizon reality. Young souls slip to the edge of sleep. Call of a dreaming sea.

Yet I dream apart. No pirate flag or treasure chart calls me from the window.
I watch & write. Tides become lines for poems, ships I send sailing out to sea.

My Ship

(After the composition by Kurt Weill)

Dawn trims the horizon near a sheltered cove and jetty. My ship
quivers as sails beat like a drum as I step on board my life, my ship.

Silver chevrons speed from the prow as the sun strikes. White triangles
haul in sky. Waves splash the echo of two words in the wake. My ship.

The young mariner morning, flushed with excitement, brushes canvas,
tips the mast red. Streamers foam white-gold in the wake of my ship.

Crests cut in a pattern of wings exhale the sea, breathe in the waves.
They steep into shape-shifters, grooming miles into time beneath my ship.

Ripples shimmer sounds into sea-wrought songs and poems.
They fill the wind, drive the furrowing spine of my ship.

Clouds stream west, draining filigrees of days into years.
Cirrus fingers set a sky-compass north for my ship.

Evenings close the sun's gold door with a click.
Sea music clinks from the ruffled spire of my ship.

The moon's skin, as the Norse say, stretches to break,
a pattern of lace from the passing ghost of my ship.

Glimmers of settlement fall away, dissolving like memory.
A lone lighthouse sweeps time & land away from my ship

How life's voyage, long or short, catches & rolls like the sea.
Sweeping cadences from a sea bird rise, then fall by my ship.

Islands rise through each night like thought, considered,
dissolved. The firmament charts a parallel path to my ship.

Calm on the surface, the unconscious thrives in the deep.
Senses roam in the dark below the white line of my ship.

At night, a kaleidoscope of stars fractures the Milky Way.
Glittering like a merry-go-round, the cosmos orbits my ship.

Beyond north, cold holds fast to ropes and sails.
Frozen mirrors reflect the icy course of my ship.

At the peak of the world, the sun skips earth like a fish.
Above, another ocean waits, sky-bound berth for my ship.

Some vessels pull against the incoming tide to eternity.
I fly to destiny in the jagged kite of my ship.

Acknowledgements

'My Ship and 'Continental Drift' appeared in *Southerly*; 'The Naming of Clouds' in the *Meuse Press anthology, Class*; 'Acorn' in the *Meuse Press anthology Humour*. 'Apron' in the W.A. Writers anthology 'Poetry D'Amour, 'Ghazal for White Cockatoos' in *The Book of Birds*; 'The Quiet American' in *Australian Poetry Anthology*.

I have been writing ghazals for about ten years. Older versions of some poems appeared in my earlier books. Some others were written as part of recent creative writing project with Tric O'Heare, for which special thanks.

Thanks also to friends in poetry both in Australia and the U.K for their support. Kerry Bourke for proofreading and to visual artist, Susan Mannion in Ireland for stimulating my decision to include the images that accompany some poems

Notes

'Bringing her home': *Dunny Race*. Australian slang for a race to the toilet

About the Author

Born in Ashfield, Sydney, Ross Donlon now lives in Castlemaine, Victoria, where he has convened poetry events for twenty years and is publisher of Mark Time Books. He has written seven books of poetry (one co-authored with Tric O'Heare) as well as five chapbooks and the educational books, *Kickstarting Poetry 1&2* (with Tric O'Heare). Winner of two international poetry competitions, the Dorothy Hewett Flagship Fellowship, the Ford Memorial Medal and the Launceston Cup, he is represented in numerous anthologies both in Australia and the U.K

He has read his work extensively both in Australia, Ireland, the U.K. and also in Norway, Romania and Poland.

A sequence of poems was made into a program on Radio National's *Poetica*.

www.ingramcontent.com/pod-product-compliance
Lightning Source LLC
Chambersburg PA
CBHW060621080526
44585CB00013B/935